You Are Alive in Christ

STONECROFT

HARVEST HOUSE PUBLISHERS
EUGENE, OREGON

Cover by Koechel Peterson & Associates, Inc., Minneapolis, Minnesota

Cover photo © Andrew Mayovskyy / iStock / Thinkstock

YOU ARE ALIVE IN CHRIST
Stonecroft Bible Studies
Copyright © 2014 by Stonecroft Ministries Inc.
Published by Harvest House Publishers
Eugene, Oregon 97402
www.harvesthousepublishers.com

ISBN 978-0-7369-5833-2 (pbk.)
ISBN 978-0-7369-5834-9 (eBook)

Printed in the United States of America

14 15 16 17 18 19 20 21 22 / VP-JH / 10 9 8 7 6 5 4 3 2 1

Contents

Acknowledgments

Stonecroft wishes to acknowledge and thank Janice Mayo Mathers for her dedication in serving the Lord through Stonecroft. Speaker, author, and member of the Board of Directors, Jan is the primary author of revised Stonecroft Bible Studies. We appreciate her love for God's Word and her love for people who need Him. Special thanks goes to the team who prayed for Jan, and those who edited, designed, and offered their creative input to make these studies accessible to all. Stonecroft is also grateful to Lucille Sollenberger, who is now with the Lord she loved and served, for the original development of this study.

Welcome to
Stonecroft Bible Studies!

It doesn't matter where you've been or what you've done...God wants to be in relationship with you. And one place He tells you about Himself is in His Word—the Bible. Whether the Bible is familiar or new to you, its contents will transform your life and bring answers to your biggest questions.

Gather with people in your communities—women, men, couples, young and old alike—and explore the completeness of the salvation that God has given us in Jesus Christ, His Son. Come to a deeper understanding of what it means to be *in Christ* and share His life, and how nothing needs to be added to our day-to-day faith: not rules or customs, not human ideas or philosophies, not religious rituals—we find completeness only in Him.

Each chapter of *You Are Alive in Christ* includes discussion questions to stir up meaningful conversation, specific Scripture verses to investigate, and time for prayer to connect with God and each other.

Discover more of God and His ways through this small-group exploration of the Bible.

Tips for Using This Study

This book includes several features that make it easy to use and helpful for your life:

- The page number or numbers given after every Bible reference are keyed to the page numbers in the *Abundant Life Bible*. This paperback Bible uses the New Living Translation, a translation in straightforward, up-to-date language. We encourage you to obtain a copy through your group leader or at stonecroft.org.

- Each chapter ends with a section called "Thoughts, Notes, and Prayer Requests." Use this space for notes or for thoughts that come to you during your group time or study, as well as prayer requests.

- In the back of the book you will find "Journal Pages"—a space available for writing down how the study is changing your life or any other personal thoughts, reactions, and reflections.

- Please make this book and study your own. We encourage you to use it and mark it in any way that helps you grow in your relationship with God!

If you find this study helpful, you may want to investigate other resources from Stonecroft. Please take a look at "Stonecroft Resources" in the back of the book or online at **stonecroft.org/store**.

stonecroft.org

A Letter to Colosse

Colossians 1:1-14

We'd been flying for hours over nothing but water, when the pilot's voice came over the intercom telling us to prepare for landing. My cousin and I looked out the window, eager to catch a glimpse of our new home, but all we could see was water. There was no land in sight. "We'll buzz the runway once to clear it of pigs and people," the pilot continued, and simultaneously the plane banked sharply to the left. Our mouths gaped in shock at the sight below us. We were staring at a mere shoestring of land lost in the vast Pacific Ocean. The atoll of Majuro, our new home, was only 30 miles long and a half mile wide—at its widest! Most of the atoll was much narrower. In fact, part of it disappeared underwater during high tide!

We'd come here as volunteer missionaries eager to find adventure, and we were not disappointed. As we exited the plane we exited life as we knew it. This primitive little island, one of hundreds that make up the nation of Micronesia, lacked the most basic of amenities we took for granted at home. The culture and living conditions were even more foreign to us than the blistering equatorial heat and humidity. That first night we hunkered down in our sparse quarters, surrounded by giant spiders, cockroaches, geckos, and mosquitoes, and we prayed for our adventure to end.

With dawn came a renewed anticipation for our adventure. In no time at all we had fallen in love with life in Micronesia. Our days were long and our responsibilities endless and challenging, but we experienced God at a deeper level than ever before. By the time we returned home we'd been forever changed.

In this study of Colossians we'll be traveling to a country different than our own and meeting people who lived under far more challenging circumstances. You are in for an adventure as we get acquainted with them and see God from their perspective. And be prepared. Like my cousin and me—you may never be the same again!

⮂

Prayer

God, you gave us the Scriptures long ago to teach us, to give us hope and encouragement as we wait patiently for your promises to be fulfilled. I know that all Scripture is inspired by you and teaches us what is true, and it makes us realize what is wrong in our lives. It corrects us when we are wrong and teaches us to do what is right. Use your Word in this study to prepare me and equip me to do every good work, for I know your Word is a lamp to guide my feet and a light for my path (Romans 15:4, page 868; 2 Timothy 3:16-17, page 915; and Psalm 119:105, page 470).

The Situation in Colosse

Ladies and gentlemen, prepare for landing! We are approaching the biblical town of Colosse, which is located in what is now the country of Turkey. The time is approximately AD 62, and although Colosse was once a larger city, it has now become smaller. Near Colosse are two larger and more prosperous cities: Laodicea and Hierapolis.

The first person we'll meet is a man named Epaphras. He had

committed his life to following Jesus and had founded a church in Colosse made up of others who shared his commitment. He grew concerned, however, because some of the people had begun dabbling in popular human philosophies or belief systems prevalent in their culture, such as mysticism, angel worship, humanism, asceticism, and legalism. They confused the simple message of the Gospel—that Jesus died for their sins—by adding in the legalism of Jewish laws, along with some pagan customs and festivals, and incorporating into this eclectic mix their own human reasoning.

All of this was counter to the teachings of Jesus and kept them from growing in their faith. It limited their ability to access all the advantages that come from a personal relationship with God. Saddest of all, it prevented them from grasping the reality of God's grace and their freedom in Christ.

Epaphras became concerned enough that he decided to seek advice from one of the top Christian leaders of the day—the apostle Paul. This meant he had to travel all the way to Rome (a difficult journey of about a thousand miles), where Paul had been imprisoned for preaching the Gospel of Jesus Christ. Epaphras and Paul discussed the problems facing the Colossians, after which Paul wrote a letter warning them of the dangers of getting involved with any kind of false teaching. The letter he wrote is what we, today, know as the New Testament book of Colossians.

As we study this letter together, I think you'll be amazed to discover just how familiar it sounds. The same philosophies that led the Colossians astray still exist today with a few different twists. And just like the Colossians, many of today's Christians are still trying to add in bits and pieces of these human philosophies to the truth of the Bible. In this verse-by-verse study of the letter to the Colossians, we will see how Paul helped them realize the danger in what they were doing and taught them how to affirm and access all the benefits of their relationship with God. In the process, we will learn how to access these same benefits for ourselves.

God Chooses Paul

Let's begin by reading Paul's greeting to the Colossians in 1:1-2 (page 902).

Paul begins by making a statement about himself— he has been chosen by God to be an apostle of Christ Jesus. Let's gain a little more information about Paul.

According to the following verses, how would you describe him?

Philippians 3:5 (page 900)

Acts 22:3 (page 851)

Tarsus was an ancient city of the Roman province of Cilicia, located in south central Turkey ten miles inland from the Mediterranean Sea. Tarsus was known for its wealth and strong education system, in which it is said to have rivaled Athens and Alexandria. Both the law of the Romans and the language and wisdom of the Greeks impacted its inhabitants.

Paul—at that time, still named Saul—was a highly educated man, having studied in Jerusalem under Gamaliel, a great Jewish teacher and member of the Sanhedrin, the highest Jewish court. Saul, deeply devoted to the Jewish religion, grew very concerned about the new and growing sect of people called Christians. Believing he was doing God's will, he persecuted them, determined to destroy Christianity once and for all. Read Acts 26:9-11 (page 854).

By his own testimony later, Saul violently opposed Christians until the day he had an encounter that radically transformed his life. Read Acts 26:12-18 (page 854).

Do you find it astounding that God chose a passionate enemy of Christianity to spread its message further afield?

Why do you think God chose a devout Jew to take this radical message to Gentiles?

It's one of the things I love most about God. He does what sometimes seems illogical from our human perspective to accomplish what is most needed. Take a moment to think of a time in your life when He used something that seemed illogical to bring about something great.

How did God's working in you affect your relationship with Him?

Saul's dramatic conversion to Christianity caused a complete one-eighty in his life. He became as passionate about following Jesus as he had been opposed to Him. He lived a life of adventure as he organized and encouraged young congregations of believers throughout Asia Minor and Europe.

Just as astonishing as Saul's conversion, however, is the fact that the Christians of that time trusted it! Think about it. Before his conversion Saul had terrorized and brutalized them, and now he's claiming to have become a believer just like they were.

If you'd lived back then, how hard would it have been for you to believe Saul's story?

Read Acts 9:13-14 (page 838) to see one man's reaction.

Ananias wasn't exactly thrilled when God asked him to go visit Saul, was he? And can you blame him? Nonetheless, Ananias did as God instructed, and Saul's amazing journey as a follower of Jesus began.

If you had lived back then, what proof of conversion would you have needed to believe Paul had truly become a Christian?

Read Galatians 1:15–2:10 (pages 890-891).

How did Paul gain approval from the first-century Christians?

Paul knew he needed the support and approval of the other apostles to most effectively share and spread the Gospel, so he went to the church in Jerusalem where Peter, James, and John were influential leaders at that time.

The believers trusted Paul and rallied behind him, and he became the most influential voice of Christianity in that time. He also became a prolific writer, authoring 13 books of the New Testament, which were actually letters he wrote to congregations and friends to train and encourage them in their faith.

If you ever have doubt that God can forgive anything, remember Paul. He went from hating Jesus to passionately loving Him. He became a dedicated, devoted Christian whose worldwide impact continues more than 2000 years later. There is no person too evil, no sin too great for God to forgive. He delights in redeeming lives!

In the first verse of Colossians, Paul calls himself an apostle. Apostles were chosen by God and spoke with God-given power and authority.

> What is one characteristic of an apostle, according to Galatians 1:1 (page 890)?

God appointed the apostles. People did not. Remember from Galatians 1:15-16 that God chose and called Paul by His grace to preach the Gospel to the Gentiles.

Christian Mentorship

Paul also mentioned a man named Timothy in Colossians 1:1. Read Acts 16:1-3 (pages 844-845) and 1 Corinthians 4:17 (page 872).

What characteristics describe Timothy in these passages?

Paul's love for Timothy is evident. Paul became his mentor, working closely with him, training him to live fully for Jesus.

Have you had someone mentor you? How did it benefit you?

Have you been a mentor to someone? What did you learn from that experience?

Timothy became a tremendous source of help and encouragement for Paul—just as Paul was for Timothy. That's one of the benefits of a mentoring relationship. Both parties benefit from the relationship. Ask God if there is someone He would like you to mentor. Jot down the name that comes to mind and pray for that person. Ask God to help you find an opportunity to make yourself available to that person.

Greeting and Gratitude

Right from the beginning, the tone of Paul's letter is warm and respectful.

How does he describe the Colossians in verse 2?

What does he ask God to give them?

This is not just a generic greeting Paul tossed their way. It got right to the heart of the matter he addressed later. Dabbling in false philosophies produces a diminished awareness of the grace of God and a distinct lack of peace. Paul immediately set to work helping them regain the ground they had lost.

Read Colossians 1:3-8 (page 902).

Do you hear the positive tone of Paul's writing? His joy and passion for serving God and his love for the Colossians are evidenced in every line.

Even though Paul was writing to correct the Colossians, there is no criticism in his words. Instead, what is the first thing he tells them in verse 3?

How does it make you feel when you know someone is praying for you?

One of the greatest gifts we can give someone is sincere prayer on their behalf. Such prayers as God leads can impact a life. For the Colossians to know that Paul—one of the key Christian leaders of the day—was praying for them would have been deeply encouraging.

What are the two reasons Paul gives in verse 4 for being thankful to God?

1.

2.

This gives us a good picture of the Colossians. They have put their faith in Christ, and their faith is evidenced by their *"love for all of God's people."* This is exactly what is supposed to happen as a result of committing our lives to Jesus. Our response to others should be love. Paul recognized this attitude in the Colossians, and we recognize it in him in the way he writes to them.

The more you read Paul's writing, the more you become aware of his immense spirit of gratitude. This gratitude has nothing to do with his external circumstances for he gave up everything to follow Jesus, and he suffered mightily as a result of it. His gratitude and joy were results of his internal condition—his relationship with God that transcended even the worst circumstance. Paul wanted the Colossians to experience the same spirit of gratitude and joy.

According to verse 6, how can we know that the Good News bears fruit all over the world?

God's wisdom is clearly guiding Paul's writing. Paul knew the Colossians' vulnerability to other philosophies that were popular in that culture. He understood the temptation to try to accommodate these philosophies; the Colossians didn't want to appear to the rest of society to be different or close-minded. Rather than condemn them, Paul told them how the Good News changed lives as it spread around the world—just as it changed their lives.

How would this affect you if you were one of the Colossians? Would it cause you to back up and re-evaluate the concessions you had started to make?

It encourages us to be a part of something alive and growing. When you feel like you're small in number and alone you can start looking around for something bigger to be a part of. We don't know if this is what caused the Colossians to begin paying more attention to other philosophies. Maybe it was pressure they felt from their culture. Maybe some of them brought beliefs or practices into their lives from before they became Christ-followers. Whatever the reason behind their compromised passion for the truth, Paul let them know they were a part of something alive and vibrant and growing.

A Marvelous Prayer

Read Colossians 1:9-12 (page 902) and record everything Paul prayed for on their behalf.

What an incredible prayer to pray for someone! Is there someone for whom you could pray these verses? Take a few minutes and do that.

Now look at the list you made. If you had to categorize your list, how would you describe it?

Paul does not ask for their physical protection. He does not ask that they will be able to pay their bills or even for healing of any in their group who are ill. No! He prays for their spiritual wisdom and growth, for fruitful lives that please the Lord, for strength and patience. He prays they will be filled with joy and a spirit of continual gratitude.

In what ways could you apply this practice in your own prayer life?

Read the last sentence of Colossians 1:12 along with verses 13 and 14 (page 902). In just a handful of words Paul reminds them of the incomprehensible gift that is theirs as children of God. Look at the words he uses: *rescued, transferred, purchased freedom, forgave!*

What did the Colossians do to earn this gift?

How does Ephesians 2:8-9 (page 896) describe this gift?

In God's immense love for us, He sent His only Son, Jesus, to die for our sins. Jesus' death and resurrection make it possible for us to have a personal relationship with God the Father. When we turn away from our sin and turn to Christ who died to save us from our sins, we become a child of God with full access to all of His promises for this life on earth plus the promise of eternal life with Him in heaven after our physical death.

If you do not have a personal relationship with God and would like to know more about this, turn to "Know God" on pages 117–119. What a great way to start this study! It will change your life in ways you never dreamed possible.

This brings us to the end of our first chapter. I suggest reading all four chapters of Colossians this week so you can obtain an idea of what we'll be studying. As you read, if any questions come to mind, jot them down and we will discuss them as we get to that point in the study.

———— *Personal Reflection and Application* ————

From this chapter,

I see…

I believe…

I will…

∾

Prayer

Lord, don't let me ever be impressed with my own wisdom. Instead, help me fear you and turn away from evil. I know that intelligent people are always ready to learn and their ears are open for knowledge, so help me to pay attention and learn good judgment, for I know you give me good guidance. Don't let me turn away from your instructions (Proverbs 3:7, page 482; Proverbs 18:15, page 493; and Proverbs 4:1-2, page 483).

Thoughts, Notes, and Prayer Requests

Christ—Creator and Savior

Colossians 1:15–2:5

When Alzheimer's disease began to impair my mother-in-law's ability to live independently, we moved her in with us. Not long after the move, I noticed that Edna's eyesight seemed to be rapidly declining. Thinking she needed a new prescription for glasses, I made an appointment with her ophthalmologist. To my surprise, after performing an extensive exam, the doctor told me her vision had not changed. "Her brain is simply no longer able to interpret what she is seeing," he said.

I thought about his diagnosis for a long time, marveling at how interdependent our body parts are. We see with our eyes, but unless our brain is functioning properly our eyes can deceive us. In a way, it's a picture of life. God designed us to live interdependently with Him. In fact, in this next section of Colossians, He is described as our head. Only when we live in unity with Him will we be able to correctly process the circumstances going on around us. The Holy Spirit within us helps us. With our "head" interpreting what our eyes see in our circumstances, the Spirit helps us realize that truly God *"causes everything to work together for the good of those who love God and are called according to his purpose for them."*

Father, it comforts me to know that you cause everything to work together for the good of those who love you and are called according to your purpose for them. Help me then to submit to you, so I will have peace and things will go well for me. Help me listen to your instructions and store them in my heart. You are my treasure, like precious silver to me! I take delight in you and look up to you (Romans 8:28, page 863, and Job 22:21-22,25-26, pages 402-403).

A Revelation of Christ

This chapter's study begins with a powerful description of Jesus Christ in Colossians 1:15-19 (page 902).

What does this passage reveal to you about Christ?

Look back over the list and contemplate what you have written down.

Why do you think it is so significant that God became visible to us through Christ?

While Jesus walked the earth in a human body, the compassion He showed, the people He befriended, and every word He spoke and action He took showed us the heart of God—*because He is God*! Jesus and God are one. The more closely we walk with Jesus, the more intimately we know God.

Revealing Christ in Our Lives

According to 2 Corinthians 3:18 (page 883), what happens as our relationship with God grows stronger?

After Jesus' resurrection, He returned to heaven, so He is no longer physically visible to us. But just as Jesus in human form made God visible, now *we* make Jesus visible through our transformed lives! Our behavior as children of God shows the world what He is like.

According to Matthew 5:14-16 (page 736), Christians are the *"light of the world."* Others will honor God because they see our good actions and behavior. Jesus states this similarly in John 13:35 (page 823) when He tells the disciples that their love for one another will show the world that they are His disciples.

How accurate would you say your reflection of God is to the people around you? How do you love the people around you?

Creator and Head of the Church

Does Colossians 1:16-17 leave any doubt as to who is responsible for the creation of the universe?

Have you ever stopped to think about the power and precision required to "hold" all of creation together (verse 17)? Think about the intelligence involved just to maintain the right amount of gravity, the earth's spin, and the exact distance from the sun and moon needed throughout the relentlessly changing conditions our planet encounters. The intelligence and power behind our existence is staggering.

What do you think it means in verse 18, *"Christ is also the head of the church, which is his body"*?

The church refers to the body of believers—every person who ever trusted in Jesus as their Savior and Lord. For Christ to be described as the head is of tremendous significance. Think of what your head does for your body. It's the control center for everything. It initiates all the actions carried on by your body. If we lived in constant awareness that Christ is our head, think of how our attitudes and actions would change! Think of how much more accurately we would reflect who God is.

Read the following passages:

Ephesians 4:15-16 (page 897)

1 Corinthians 12:25-27 (page 877)

In those verses, what godly qualities are seen in the unified body?

Reconciled to God the Father Through God the Son

It is a picture of beneficial unity. It is a picture of health and vitality that occurs as we determine by God's grace to live in a way that makes Christ visible to the world around us.

Read Colossians 1:19-20 (page 902).

Paul makes it clear again that Jesus and God are one, with the same attributes and deserving of the same honor.

Read John 5:22-24 (page 813).

Jesus is fully God, and He provided us with eternal life when He died for our sins.

What does verse 24 say about those who believe this?

We will *never be condemned* for our sins. We already have eternal life! Colossians 1:20-22 (page 902) explains this more fully.

Reconciliation speaks of a change of relationship between God and humans.

When Jesus came to earth and died for our sins, what was reconciled?

What is the result of our reconciliation?

Romans 5:8-10 (page 860) says the very same thing.

Jesus was fully innocent (sinless) when He gave His life for us, and because of His death, we, who were once separated from Him by our sin, are now fully innocent as well. *"Without a single fault,"* it says. Only God, whose love for us is perfect, could have made this possible. Only He could have found a way for us to be able to reflect His image here on earth so others will be drawn to Him.

Human Philosophies vs. God's Truth

In the next verse, Colossians 1:23 (page 902), Paul urges the Colossian Christians to do three things. What are they?

1.

2.

3.

What are some things that might cause us to *"drift away"* from God's truth?

Remember, the Colossians were dabbling in human philosophies. They were spending time learning about these philosophies, which led them to be accommodating of them, which undermined their foundation of truth. There is nothing wrong with learning about different philosophies or religions in order to better understand the distinctiveness of our own relationship with Christ. Still, we should not make accommodations for a philosophy not fully aligned with God's Word. If we are not careful, we may make accommodations that can bring confusion to our understanding of the power of the Gospel and the effective work Christ completed on the cross.

Suffering on Behalf of the Truth

In the final verses of Colossians 1, Paul's remarkable attitude as a result of his relationship with God is again evident. Read Colossians 1:24-29 (pages 902-903).

Why is Paul glad to suffer?

He counts it a privilege when his suffering is a result of his belief in Jesus Christ. He takes his responsibility to serve other believers seriously—even if it lands him in prison. If he can look at his suffering as a privilege, this means it is possible for the Colossians to do the same. Can you see how his words must have encouraged them and spurred them on in their faith?

Paul experienced extreme persecution as a result of sharing his faith. Read 1 Corinthians 4:11-13 (page 872).

How did Paul respond to bad treatment?

He reflected the love of God that transformed his life. The truth is, when we commit our lives to God, sometimes we suffer as a result. Read 2 Timothy 3:12 (page 915) and Matthew 5:11-12 (page 736).

Persecution comes in many different forms—intimidation, racism, slander, mocking, and so on. In some countries, persecution comes through much harsher means: imprisonment, torture, and even death. Whatever persecution we experience, our response should be like Paul's—trusting God in the situation and reflecting His transformational love. God promises He will never leave us alone in it.

What do the following passages have in common?

2 Corinthians 4:8-10 (page 884)

Matthew 28:18-20 (page 760)

Think about that for a minute. God promises He will *never* fail or abandon us! Such dependability is worthy of our trust, don't you think?

Holding Firmly to Christ

Read Colossians 2:1-3 (page 903).

Imagine learning that one of the top Christian leaders was agonizing over you in prayer. How would you feel about that?

Personally, it would give me a greater sense of how important it is to maintain my commitment to God—not just for myself, but for God's glory and for everyone in my sphere of influence.

The church in nearby Laodicea was also struggling. Paul wants the Christians in both cities to feel connected by God's love so they can encourage each other to stay firm in their commitment to Him.

What does Paul say is hidden in Christ?

"All the treasures of wisdom and knowledge"—it is all found in Christ, and He will share it with us as we walk with Him.

Some of the false teachers who were gaining the attention of the Colossians had long lists of rules to follow, complicated formulas for fulfillment that brought confusion into their lives. Paul wanted them to know that all they needed was Christ. In Him they would find all the wisdom and knowledge they needed for this life and for eternity.

Read Colossians 2:4-5 (page 903).

In spite of the seriousness of what Paul writes about, his words are warm and his praise is sincere and encouraging as he warns the Colossians about the people who are deceiving them with good-sounding, convincing arguments. Such people are all around us today as well.

Read the following verses and note what they say about this:

2 Timothy 4:3-5 (page 915)

1 Timothy 4:1-2 (page 911)

Romans 16:17-18 (page 869)

The message is clear: be on guard against human philosophies. Stay away! Keep a clear mind! One of the most common teachings—one that has been around through all of time—teaches that there are many paths that lead to God. It sounds good and logical though it comes from the lips of false teachers and is a lie that leads to death because it denies the sacrifice Jesus made for us (1 Timothy 2:5-6, page 910).

What are some other myths floating around that sound good but contradict the truth of God found in the Bible?

Read the following passages. What are some different ways we can determine if something is false teaching?

1 John 4:1-3 (page 943)

John 14:26 (pages 823-824)

2 Timothy 3:16 (page 915)

2 Thessalonians 3:14-15 (page 909)

Remember we read that in Christ we have access to all wisdom and knowledge. The Holy Spirit living within us helps us *know* when we hear the truth. The more closely we walk with God—praying, studying the Bible, and obeying its teaching—the more certain we become of what is truth and what isn't. He has given us all we need to protect us from being deceived. Only in Him do we know the truth.

————— *Personal Reflection and Application* —————

From this chapter,

I see…

I believe…

I will…

Prayer

Lord, teach me your ways so I may live according to your truth! Grant me purity of heart so I may honor you. For your Word is alive and powerful. It is sharper than the sharpest two-edged sword, cutting between soul and spirit, between joint and marrow. It exposes my innermost thoughts and desires. So let me hold firmly to what I believe, because Jesus understands my weaknesses—He faced all of the same testings I do, yet He did not sin. I know I can come boldly to you, God, and I will receive your mercy and find grace to help me when I need it most (Psalm 86:11, page 453, and Hebrews 4:12,14b-16, page 922).

Thoughts, Notes, and Prayer Requests

_____

_____

_____

_____

_____

_____

_____

_____

_____

_____

_____

_____

_____

3

Complete in Christ

Colossians 2:6-15

I pulled the letter from the mailbox with a sigh, sure it was just another rejection letter from a publisher. Tearing open the envelope, I pulled out the form letter. "We are pleased to inform you we have accepted your book…"

Flinging the rest of the mail in the air, I danced into the house waving the letter above my head. "They accepted it!" I yelled. "I am now officially an author!" My husband and sons came running to join in my celebration, knowing what a huge milestone this was for me. My first book had just been purchased for publication.

I laid the contract on the kitchen counter and stared in wonder. A publisher found my work worthy of publication. That piece of paper covered with legal mumbo jumbo identified and accepted me as an author. What a wonderful word—*accepted*. What a pleasure to be identified with something I held in high regard.

That contract does not solely define my identity. My wedding band identifies me as a wife, my glasses identify I have vision problems. Other identities, such as being a mother, an American, or a lover of green, are not as visible. However, my most significant identity point is that I am a child of God. Although I have no contract to frame and hang on my wall as proof, the unfathomable truth is, on the day I trusted Jesus by God's gift of faith, I received Jesus as my Savior, and the Creator of the universe accepted me as His child. That's an identity worth dancing about!

∽

Prayer

Oh Father, I see how very much you love me that you call me your child, and that is what I am! Because I believe in Jesus and have accepted Him, you have given me the right to become your child. This means I am a new person. My old life is gone, and my new life has begun. Now I am your masterpiece, created anew in Christ Jesus so I can do the good things you planned for me long ago (1 John 3:1a, page 942; John 1:12, page 809; 2 Corinthians 5:17, page 884; and Ephesians 2:10, page 896).

The Indwelling Christ

The first two chapters of Colossians reveal a sacred secret not revealed in the Old Testament. If you recall, we read in Colossians 1:26 (page 903) that *"this message was kept secret for centuries and generations past, but now it has been revealed to God's people…"* The secret is *"Christ lives in you"*—He lives in Jews and Gentiles, in everyone who believes.

This is a powerful, transformative truth—Christ lives within us—equipping us for every challenge we face. But some of the Colossian Christians were being misled and confused about this. They were attempting to understand the mystery of God and His salvation by adding their own explanation to the truth. Without realizing what they were doing, they were saying that Christ's death for us was not enough. They were adding human philosophy and rituals to God's divine truth. They were misinterpreting Scripture and taking it out of context in order to reduce His truth to fit their human logic.

We do the same thing today. Our human way of thinking resists the idea that God's salvation is free and that we can do nothing to earn it. We use faulty logic to invent ways to earn His acceptance. We create rules and procedures to make us feel good about our spirituality instead of accepting the simple but profound truth that His love for us took care of it all.

Read Hebrews 4:14-16 (page 922).

> This is an incredible passage for several different reasons. First of all, why do you think it says that Jesus understands our weaknesses?

This is something we often don't take into account. Jesus fully identifies with us. He fully understands what our life is like because He lived here on earth under the limitations of humanity. It's one thing, for example, to say to a homeless person, "I can imagine how hard life is for you," and an entirely different thing to say, "I know what your life is like because I've been homeless too." Jesus isn't sympathetic to us because He can *imagine* our life. He is sympathetic because He has *lived* our life. He faced temptations, challenges, and heartaches as we do. He knows from personal experience what it is like.

> How does verse 16 say we can come to God?

Not hat in hand, shoulders slumped, but boldly, with confidence, because we know God is gracious. He will help us because He loves us and has designed us for good—His good.

What will we find at His throne?

Ponder those words for a moment: *mercy, grace.* Mercy means we do not receive the judgment or punishment we deserve. Grace is God's favor, which we cannot earn or deserve.

What do these terms mean to you personally? How do they comfort or reassure you?

Rooted in Christ, Who Is Our Life

Paul urges the Colossians to hold firm to what they believe because it is God's truth. He doesn't want their belief to be poisoned by human philosophies. Read Colossians 2:6-7 (page 903).

What three things does he tell them to do?

1.

2.

3.

Jesus Christ doesn't want to be only our helper. He wants to be our *life*! He doesn't want us to work *for* Him. He wants to work *through* us, which happens when He lives *in* us. A complete life transformation occurs as we follow Him, build our life on Him, and let our roots grow down deep in Him. This happens as we do what the following verses teach us.

As you read the verses, note what they say.

John 15:4-5 (page 824)

Romans 6:12-13 (page 861)

1 Corinthians 15:58 (page 880)

Philippians 4:5-6 (page 901)

This is how we will become rooted and stay rooted in Christ. Just as a tree receives its life from the earth in which its roots are deeply established, so we receive our life from God, becoming firmly established in our faith and rooted in Christ—so no false teaching will uproot us.

What two things does Colossians 2:7 say will be the result of becoming rooted in Christ?

1.

2.

Note that Paul specifies where our faith grows strong. It grows strong *"in the truth."* In other words, we will not be deceived by any of the good-sounding but wrong philosophies or doctrines floating around.

The second result is that we will *"overflow with thankfulness"*!

How does God produce thankfulness in you?

He desires that our lives overflow with thankfulness. He wants us to live through and in all circumstances with an attitude of thanksgiving that comes from being rooted in Him—the One who loved us enough to die for us, the One who holds our lives in His hands.

We Are Complete

Read Colossians 2:8-10 (page 903).

We have everything we need in Christ. In Him alone we are complete. While philosophies and views today try to capture our attention, if we lean into them we will always come up empty because they cannot satisfy our deepest longing. They are at best incomplete and, candidly, a distraction. But with Christ we experience all of who God is.

What do you do to avoid being distracted by human philosophies or thinking?

The truth that comes from God, the truth we read about in the Bible, is that we find all we need to live a complete and full life in Christ. He is the source from whom courage, wisdom, and strength flow. If we are in union with Him, we have all we need. In Him we find purpose, wisdom, love, power, grace, patience, and peace. In Him we find completion. We have complete salvation, forgiveness, and victory.

We Are Completely Identified with Christ

Read Colossians 2:11-15 (page 903).

Physical circumcision was an important and permanent identifier for Jewish males. It was the covenant sign of ethnic belonging and biological lineage. Paul likens our conversion to a spiritual circumcision, in which our sinful nature is cut away and we are from that point on identified with Christ.

What did Christ do for us, according to verse 14?

Canceled! Paid in full! Forgiven! Is there a more wonderful concept than that? To know we deserve death but instead are given life. Oh, what magnificent love God has for us!

What does Romans 5:8 (page 860) say?

Other translations of this verse say God "proved" or "demonstrated" His love for us. God's love for us is undeniable.

What does Colossians 2:12 liken our transformation to?

Our salvation is like being resurrected from the dead! In fact, it *is* a resurrection from the dead. God intervened on our behalf when we were spiritually dead. The Holy Spirit convicted us of our need for Jesus. He opened our heart to trust Him. He gave us life!

According to Colossians 2:13, who makes believers alive?

Verse 14 says that God *"canceled the record of the charges against us and took it away by nailing it to the cross."*

When Paul described in verse 15 the victory that is the result of Jesus' death on the cross, he might have been referring to the image of a victorious Roman conqueror parading his defeated enemies through the city. The power of Satan and his dark forces was permanently defeated, and we are alive in Christ as a result!

Personal Reflection and Application

From this chapter,

I see...

I believe...

I will...

Prayer

God, you are so rich in kindness and grace that you purchased my freedom with the blood of your Son and forgave my sins. Now there is no condemnation for me because I belong to Christ Jesus. You have removed my sin as far from me as the east is from the west and you have compassion for me. You trample my sins under your feet and throw them into the depths of the ocean (Ephesians 1:7, page 895; Romans 8:1, page 862; Psalm 103:12-13 page 460; and Micah 7:19, page 708).

Thoughts, Notes, and Prayer Requests

4

Christ Is Supreme

Colossians 2:16–3:4

When they were teenagers, my son and his friend bought a car together—an unlicensed, beat-up piece of junk that could only be driven on our property. They convertible-ized it with a blowtorch and, donning goggles, took off in a cloud of dust across our acreage. That night, fearing for their safety, my husband slipped out and pulled a few wires to disable the car.

The next afternoon the boys wrestled with the engine for several hours, trying to figure out why it wouldn't start. Steve and I smiled, confident the threat of bodily harm had passed. Just then the engine roared to life. "How on earth…?" Steve leapt to his feet as the boys drove around the house waving triumphantly. I could not understand how they derived pleasure driving the heap of junk in a circle on our property when they both had nice cars they could drive anywhere.

That night, Steve sneaked out to pull a few more wires. Two days later the car was again running. "Good grief!" Steve exclaimed. "How do they keep fixing it?" The grudging admiration in his voice was unmistakable.

It took four attempts before Steve finally outwitted the boys. Admitting defeat, they pushed the car to its permanent resting place beside our shed. Each time I see its rusting skeleton, it reminds me of my spiritual journey. God disabled the power of sin in my life long ago, but I have a tendency to fiddle around with the wires of old attitudes and habits until they fire up again. They cause me to spin around in dusty circles of stunted growth, when all the time God calls me out into the wide-open spaces of abundant life. Just like my son finally walked away from his going-nowhere car, I need to walk away from my going-nowhere attitudes and habits.

Prayer

Father, I have discovered this principle of life—that when I want to do what is right, I inevitably do what is wrong. I love your law with all my heart, but there is another power within me that is at war with my mind. Thank you, God, that the answer is in Jesus Christ my Lord. Help me to not copy the behavior and customs of this world, but instead let you transform me into a new person by changing the way I think. Then I will learn to know your will for me, which is good and pleasing and perfect (Romans 7:21-23a,25a, page 862, and Romans 12:2, page 866).

Adding to Christ Subtracts from Our Faith

We concluded the last chapter with the marvelous truth that Satan is permanently defeated! God triumphed over sin for all time, and when we trust Jesus as our Savior we have His life and power flowing through us. We also talked about how the Colossians were beginning to embrace some incorrect human philosophies, just as we are sometimes tempted to do. False teachers were telling them that Christ alone was not enough, that they needed Christ plus legalism, Christ plus mysticism, Christ plus asceticism, Christ plus humanism, and so on. Yet Christ is sufficient. Reread Colossians 2:10.

We continue the discussion with Paul addressing some of the specific things that were confusing the Colossian Christians.

The Problem of Laws and Customs

Read Colossians 2:16-17 (page 903).

Under the Old Testament Law, there were certain foods the people were not supposed to eat. But when Jesus came, He taught that it's not what goes into our mouths that causes us to sin, but what comes out of our mouths—words that wound and debase (Matthew 15:11, page 746). Food was not the issue. Food had nothing to do with winning God's approval.

Read 1 Corinthians 8:8 (page 874).

This is an example of how people add to the truth. We can make our relationship with God about rules rather than the grace He offers. Thankfully, He knows our heart.

Holy days and festivals were also confusing some of the people in Colosse. For example, the Old Testament Law commanded that people observe the weekly Sabbath, the seventh day of the week (Exodus 20:8-11, page 59). In the New Testament, Christians began worshipping God on the "Lord's Day," the first day of the week, to commemorate the resurrection of Jesus Christ from the dead (John 20:1,19-20, page 828).

Also, religious festivals and new moons related to Temple sacrifices under the old Jewish animal-sacrifice system. Paul wanted the Christians to know that these laws and customs that once formed the basis of Jewish life and loyalty to God were no longer necessary. These things only prepared the way for God's revelation of Himself in Jesus Christ. Now that Jesus had come, the "shadow" or precursor of His coming, these laws and holidays, were no longer necessary.

The Problem of "Religious" People

It wasn't just laws and customs that were distracting the Colossians from the truth of God. People who claimed religious superiority did as well. Read Colossians 2:18-19 (page 903).

Some people in that day claimed to have had special visions and followed practices that were supposed to give them special knowledge that made them more religious than others. Some were worshipping angels instead of, or along with, God.

What does God say about this in Exodus 20:4 (page 59)?

We are to worship only God—not angels, not other people, not anyone but God Himself.

People who claim to have superior knowledge through certain religious practices believe they can discover the true meaning of life by their own efforts and set themselves up as spiritual leaders.

What did Paul say about these people in verses 18 and 19 (page 903)?

The terrible result is they lead people away from God. God is the only true source of life and growth.

The Problem of Special Rules and Practices

Read Colossians 2:20-23 (page 903).

Verse 20 asks a key question. How would you answer it?

There are various answers to that question, but verse 23 sums it up succinctly. What does it say?

Doing something often makes us feel like we are earning God's free gift. It gives us an illusion of deserving what God has done for us. But such actions accomplish nothing! They do nothing to help us conquer our evil desires.

What do the following verses say God provided?

Galatians 5:22-23 (page 893)

Romans 8:1-3 (page 862)

What is the area you need to work on most?

What are some practical steps you can take to strengthen this area?

Each of these practices is interwoven with the others. If you work on improving one—for instance, seeking God with all of your heart—the others will be strengthened as well.

Which of the fruit listed in the Galatians verses do you see lacking in your life?

The Focus of Our New Life

Read Colossians 3:1-4 (page 903).

Living for Christ first begins in our minds. As we fill our minds with the truth of God, our thought process then determines our actions. By His grace, we behave in a way that glorifies Him and benefits others. The battle between our flesh and our spirit becomes less intense.

Read Romans 12:2 (page 866).

What will God do for you?

Don't you love the word *transform*? The Greek word is *metamorphoo*, which means to change, to transform, or to transfigure. That's what happens when we focus on and yield to God. He changes our thinking so that we become more like Him.

What do the following verses say about our focus?

Hebrews 12:1-2 (page 927)

Matthew 6:33 (page 738)

How does Hebrews 12:2 (page 927) refer to Jesus?

Think about that! Jesus—Almighty God, Creator of the world—is *your* champion! God Himself cheers you on. Even more wonderful, as you fix your eyes on Him, He infuses you with all the endurance and power and strength you need to cross the finish line as a victor. He is in the process of making you perfect just as He is perfect!

And what did Matthew 6:33 say God would be doing in the process?

Contemplate that for a minute. In Him we have everything we need! Nothing is lacking. We don't have to add to it; we don't have to be more or do more. When we fix our eyes on Him we have it all.

Again and again the Bible tells us that when we become a follower of Jesus, we are no longer controlled by a sin nature.

The following verses offer just a few examples:

Colossians 3:3 (page 903)

Romans 6:1-2 (page 861)

1 Peter 2:24 (page 935)

Galatians 2:19-20 (page 891)

How would you summarize what you just read?

How would you answer the question asked in Romans 6:2?

The battle is won or lost in our minds. That's where we decide, by God's grace, what will control us—God or sin. Are we going to believe His Word—that we are dead to sin—and let His power flow through us, or do we keep reconnecting the wires to our former ways, which limit us to living in dusty circles of defeat?

Being with Christ When He Is Revealed

Colossians 3:3 talked about our being hidden in Christ.

What does Colossians 3:4 (page 903) say?

Right now, our lives make Christ visible to the world, but one day He will return and everyone will see Him. Read 1 Thessalonians 4:16-18 (page 906).

What a wonderful event for all who have committed their lives to Christ! Imagine finally seeing face-to-face our beloved Savior who gave up His life for us. Imagine at last living with Him in a new home that's beyond our wildest dreams.

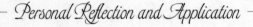

Personal Reflection and Application

From this chapter,

I see...

I believe...

I will...

Prayer

Lord, help me stay alert! Help me watch out for my great enemy, the devil. I know that he prowls around like a roaring lion, looking for someone to devour. Help me to stand firm against him and be strong in my faith. I will humble myself before you and will resist the devil so he will flee from me. I know I am a citizen of heaven where you live, and I am eagerly waiting for you to return as my Savior. You will take my weak mortal body and change it into a glorious body like your own, using the same power with which you will bring everything under your control (1 Peter 5:8-9a, page 937; James 4:7, page 932; and Philippians 3:20-21, page 901).

Thoughts, Notes, and Prayer Requests

Christ and the New Life

Colossians 3:5-17

The rain pelted against my windshield with such force that my car wipers couldn't keep up. I peered anxiously through the torrent, trying to stay on my side of the road as the winter storm battered my car. It was late at night, and I still had an hour of driving before reaching my destination. Suddenly my headlights went out, and simultaneously the engine stopped. Dread settled over me as I coasted to the side of the road, where the inky darkness engulfed me. I was at least 20 miles from the closest town.

"God, I need your help," I whispered. Immediately an old, dark-colored van lumbered to a stop several hundred feet in front of me. A large, powerfully built man in black clothes stepped out and walked toward my car. As I watched him approach I repeated over and over, "I'm in your hands, God. I praise you and I trust you."

As it happened, the man had noticed my headlights dimming several miles back and assumed correctly my alternator was going out. He stayed behind my car until it stopped and then pulled over too, parking far enough in front of me to give me plenty of time to observe him. He lived in the very next town and knew where to have my car towed. He delivered me safely to my motel, and as I thanked him for his help, he explained why he had stopped. "Last week, my wife's car broke down and no one stopped to help her," he said. "I told the Lord the next time I passed a car on the side of the road I would stop."

Prayer

God, I know how much you love me, and I have put my trust in your love. You are love, and as I live in love I live in you, and you live in me. I know that you hold me by my hand. You are the Lord my God, and you tell me not to be afraid because you are here to help me (1 John 4:16, page 943, and Isaiah 41:13, page 548).

Whenever we read God's Word, truth is revealed. As we put this knowledge into action, our lives change. The man who stopped to help me had been changed as a result of his belief in God. That's why he willingly risked helping a stranger. My life changed as a result of God, and focusing on Him fills me with peace even in my helplessness. He changes lives!

Actions and Attitudes That Reveal Our New Life in Christ

In the last chapter, we were challenged to focus our minds on God. In this chapter Paul gets very specific about what we should avoid as followers of Christ and what we should embrace. He begins by addressing some personal, internal issues. Read Colossians 3:5 (page 903).

"Lurking" is a perfect word for destructive thoughts and desires, isn't it? Such things do lurk in the dark corners of our mind and adversely influence our decisions and behaviors if we don't put them to death. *The Message* paraphrase of this verse says, *"That's a life shaped by things and feelings instead of by God."*

"Christian renewal is not some cosmetic overhaul of our sinful personalities. We do not simply add on a veneer of Christian values that only laminates our old nature and its value system." [1]
— David Garland

We make a conscious decision not to simply suppress evil *actions*, but to recognize even the evil *desires* that pop into our minds. Not in our own strength, but by the power of the Holy Spirit within us, we kill any thought of such evil.

Our surrender to the omnipotent power of God supplies what is needed for impossible things to happen in our lives. He can destroy any physical or emotional addictions that hold us captive, and He can set us truly free (John 8:36, page 817).

From the following verses, describe the areas Paul exhorts us to avoid—"*put to death.*"

Colossians 3:5-9 (page 903)

Ephesians 5:3-5 (page 897)

Romans 2:5-9 (page 858)

Though God makes us into new creatures when we become Christians, we still battle daily in choosing godly attitudes and actions. Paul's struggle with this was recorded in Romans 7:18-25 (page 862). He admits that sometimes when he wanted to do right, he did wrong. Sometimes he allowed his sin nature to control him instead of allowing himself to be controlled by the Spirit and to live in Christ's freedom and power.

Controlled by Christ, Surrounded by the Love of God the Father

Read Romans 6:11-14 (page 861).

What would it look like if we believed and lived as though this could be done—that we could be controlled by Christ rather than by our sin?

Do you sincerely want what God wants for you? Take some time right now to assess the attitude of your heart. Have you ever thought, *"I want this whether God approves or not?"*

If you discovered this unwilling attitude in your heart, I urge you to repent and seek God's perfect wisdom. James 4:17 (page 932) says that it is a sin to not do what you know is right.

Read 1 John 1:9 (page 941).

Our God is faithful and just. He will always forgive us when we confess our sins. Confess means admit the sin and agree with God about it. As great and fearsome as God's anger is, His mercy is even greater. Read Psalm 103:8-14 (page 460).

It's an incredible passage of Scripture—a great one to memorize and meditate on. Did you notice that twice it referred to God's *"unfailing love"* for us? Think about the implications of that phrase.

What exceptions does it leave room for?

What does it mean to you to know that God's love for you is unfailing?

Do you have trouble really believing God feels this way about you? If so, take a moment and tell Him that. Ask Him to help you comprehend the depth of the love He feels for you.

What other verse or phrase did you find comforting or reassuring in this passage?

God's mercy and understanding is far, far greater than any of our sins. He fully understands our weaknesses, and He makes accessible all we need to overcome them. Our part is, by His grace, to focus on Him and intentionally keep removing ourselves from what tempts us—to lock ourselves in His loving, power-infusing embrace.

Treating Others in a Way That Matches Our New Life

The next area Paul addresses has to do with habits and attitudes in regard to our interaction with others. Some of these have become such a part of us we don't think of them as being sinful.

Read Colossians 3:7-10 (page 903) and list the six things it specifically mentions.

1.

2.

3.

4.

5.

6.

What do you see as the difference between anger and rage?

Although one seems more extreme than the other, both spring from the same source: our old nature that should no longer rule us. What about malicious behavior? How would you define that?

It's not pleasant to think that we have behaved maliciously, but consider synonyms such as *spiteful* or *hateful*. Who in your life, if anyone, might accuse you of such behavior recently?

The admonitions against dirty language and lying speak for themselves, and both are derogatory behaviors that grieve the Holy Spirit. Read Ephesians 4:29 (page 897).

Paul warns against all behaviors and attitudes that displease God and hinder our fellowship with Him and demean others. He urges us to purge these things from our lives. While this is for our own good and the good of others, the most important reason is so we'll be an accurate reflection of Christ to the world and bring Him glory.

The Message paraphrase defines our old nature as a *"filthy set of ill-fitting clothes,"* and our new nature as *"a new wardrobe. Every item of your new way of life is custom-made by the Creator, with his label on it"*

(Colossians 3:9-10). That's a great way of putting it. Once we commit our lives to Christ, our old lifestyle becomes ill-fitting and unsatisfying. Now we wear custom-made clothes designed by God Himself, with His personal label. That enables us, because we are clothed in His power, to reflect His image. How wonderful!

Seeing Other Christians as Christ's Home

Read Colossians 3:11 (page 903).

In what ways would you personally like to see this truth lived out in your life? Among your friends?

"Christ is all that matters, and he lives in all of us." God sees no distinction among those who commit their lives to Him. We are all equal regardless of ethnicity, religion, gender, IQ, education level, political affiliation, profession, or bank-account balance.

We will never look alike physically, but if we are living according to our new nature we should be behaving and thinking alike—accurately reflecting the image of Jesus who lives within us, making Him look appealing to everyone around us who does not yet have a relationship with Him.

In the first 11 words of Colossians 3:12, Paul reminds the believers of three truths about themselves.

What are those truths?

1.

2.

3.

It is only because of God's grace (which can't be earned) that He chose us, cleansed us to make us holy, and loves us unconditionally.

Harmony Among the Holy People God Loves

What does the previous paragraph mean practically? Read Colossians 3:12-15 (pages 903-904) and describe the different attributes we should possess as followers of Jesus.

Though a bit daunting, each attribute characterizes our new nature. The more we focus on God, the more these define us. The natural differences among us work together in unity rather than discord.

Which characteristic do you find the most challenging and why?

Did you notice the last one? *"Always be thankful."* I think it's interesting that it is last. We talked about this earlier—that if we concentrate on cultivating an attitude of thankfulness regardless of our circumstances, all the other characteristics become more apparent. When your heart is full of gratitude, it doesn't leave room for unforgiveness, impatience, or other negative characteristics.

One of the most helpful means of developing an attitude of thankfulness is to take time each day to list a few things for which you thank God. This helps turn your thoughts in the right direction. I find this habit especially helpful when people or circumstances cause me angst. I deliberately list several good things about them each day.

Verses 14 and 15 are significant. What binds us in perfect harmony?

Where do we find the peace to rule our hearts?

We do not have to—and in fact, can't—develop these attributes on our own. Jesus living in us is the only way we can experience a level of life ruled by love and peace. These attributes can never be gained by any other means, including all the other good-sounding human philosophies floating around back then or even today.

The Peace That Comes from Christ

One of the greatest and most comforting gifts God gives us is a sense of peace that can pervade every circumstance that comes into our lives. Such peace is only accessible through Him. The Amplified Bible puts Colossians 3:15 this way:

> *Let the peace (soul harmony which comes) from Christ rule (act as umpire continually) in your hearts [deciding and settling with finality all questions that arise in your minds, in that peaceful state] to which as [members of Christ's] one body you were also called [to live].*

Like vehicles which have warning lights to tell drivers when something is wrong, our unsettled hearts may be the Holy Spirit's warning that we are heading in the wrong direction, even in our thoughts. Believers should pay close attention when their normally peaceful heart is disturbed.

What do the following verses say about this peace?

John 14:27 (page 824)

John 16:33 (page 825)

Philippians 4:6-7 (page 901)

Think about the last verse you read. God's peace *exceeds* what we can understand. It *guards* our hearts and our minds. When circumstances devastate our lives, when our hearts feel permanently broken, His peace is able to infiltrate the devastation and set up a barrier around our hearts and minds. And since He is God, He knows how to do that. Think of a time when you have experienced His unexplainable peace. Please share.

Representatives Filled with the Message About Christ

Read Colossians 3:16 (page 904).

What all are we supposed to do with everything we know about Christ?

In other words, we should saturate ourselves with His teaching. We should use it as our source for teaching and counseling each other because of its trustworthy wisdom.

Did you notice what attitude was brought up again? Paul continues to emphasize the importance of gratitude. An attitude of thankfulness can often crowd out attitudes that oppose the teaching of Christ.

Colossians 3:17 (page 904) sums up what Paul is saying to the Colossians.

What did he call them?

Whatever we do, whatever we say, never forget that we represent Jesus on earth. Our actions and words paint a picture to the world of what Jesus is like—every place we go, everything we do, every word we speak. Our behavior and attitude within our families represent Christ. Our behavior and attitude at work and school represent Christ. Our behavior and attitude in stores and restaurants, gyms and theaters, parks and playgrounds—whether we're having a good day or bad day, we are a window to the world of what Christ is like.

Giving Thanks to God Through Christ

At the risk of belaboring a point, what does the last part of verse 17 say?

Paul would not keep saying this if it wasn't important. What do the following verses say about giving thanks?

Ephesians 5:20 (page 898)

1 Thessalonians 5:18 (page 907)

I have a friend who hated everything about her job—the people, the pressure, the location of her office, and the responsibilities assigned to her. When things reached the unbearable point she came over to have coffee and to vent. On one visit I suggested that each night before leaving work, she e-mail me five things she was grateful for that day. She agreed to try.

Barely two weeks passed before fellow employees started noticing a change in her. "You seem happier these days," one man said. People started stopping by her office to say hi, and her boss moved her into a nicer office!

There is a reason Paul repeated the importance of developing an attitude of thankfulness. It changes our lives; it positively impacts the people around us. Most important of all, it pleases God and brings Him glory while giving people a correct image of Jesus.

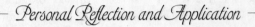

Personal Reflection and Application

From this chapter,

I see…

I believe…

I will…

Prayer

Lord, I want to imitate you in everything I do because I am your dear child. Help me to live a life filled with love, following the example of Christ, who loved me and offered Himself as a sacrifice for me. Because I belong to you, the power of your life-giving Spirit has freed me from the power of sin that leads to death. Help me not be dominated by my sinful nature, thinking about sinful things, but let me be controlled by the Holy Spirit, thinking about things that please you and lead me to life and peace (Ephesians 5:1-2, page 897, and Romans 8:2,5-6, page 862).

Thoughts, Notes, and Prayer Requests

Christlike Relationships

Colossians 3:18–4:1

A friend of ours had a small welding business that had been in the family for three generations. When he took it over from his father, he felt considerable pressure to maintain the business successfully. He was excited when he had enough work to hire an employee. Bill trained his new employee in all aspects of welding, and he worked for Bill for several years. Then one day he announced he was starting his own welding business in the same small town where his employer lived.

Bill was concerned about how the competition would affect his business, but he decided to encourage the man and help him get started, even passing along jobs he couldn't get to in a timely manner. Bill hired another employee, and a couple of years later the same thing happened. Over time he trained four employees, each of whom eventually moved on to start his own welding business in the same area. Every time Bill worried he'd be put out of business, but he set his mind to help them and prayed for their success.

In this chapter we will discuss various relationships—including the employer-employee relationship. Key to success in each of these relationships is an attitude of humility, a willingness to seek the best for the other person. When we do that, God promises to bless us.

Through Bill's years in business God kept that promise. When the economy was good there was plenty of work for everyone. When the economy was bad, the new welding companies went out of business, every time funneling just enough work Bill's way for him to get by. And in every case, his former employees have remained his good friends.

Prayer

    Lord, help me not to look out only for my own interests, but to take an interest in others too. Let me never forget that if I give, I will receive. My gift will return to me in full—pressed down, shaken together to make room for more, running over, and poured into my lap. Help me to do good and share with those in need, because the sacrifice pleases you (Philippians 2:4, page 900; Luke 6:38, page 786; and Hebrews 13:16, page 929).

You've probably noticed by now that although we are going verse by verse through Colossians, we haven't been paying attention to the chapter breaks. The Bible wasn't always divided into chapters and verses. While the words of the Scriptures are Holy Spirit-inspired, the chapter and verse divisions were devised by people to aid in studying. Sometimes the divisions broke up the subjects being discussed. For this reason, some of the contemporary versions of the Bible supplement the chapter-and-verse division with paragraph arrangements, which further help with study.

Relationships Among People Who Are in Christ

Today we will look at an emotionally volatile passage of Scripture that deals with three types of relationships. Let's read the entire passage. Then we'll go back and take it apart. Read Colossians 3:18–4:1 (page 904).

This section of Scripture stirs up a variety of emotions. Three kinds of relationships are discussed—husband and wife, parent and child, and master and slave. In our society today we would consider the latter an employer and employee relationship.

Woven into each of these relationships are words like *submit, love, obey, please*, and *serve*. Let's begin by taking a look at the word *submit*.

Considering the Word Submit

Merriam-Webster defines *submit* as "to yield to governance or authority." The Greek word *hypotasso* "does not convey some innate inferiority, but is used for a modest, cooperative demeanor that puts others first." [2] We've talked repeatedly in this study about the importance of attitude and how attitude determines behavior. To understand the concept of submission, we need to view it both as an attitude and a behavior.

Let's look at who God tells us we should submit to in the following verses.

Job 22:21 (page 402)

Romans 13:1 (page 866)

Ephesians 5:21 (page 898)

So we are to submit to God, governing authorities, and each other.

According to Job 22:21, what is the result of submission to God?

Peace is the result of submission. An attitude of submission means you are willing to set aside your own desires for someone else's benefit.

How does Philippians 2:3 (page 900) complement this?

Let that sink in for a minute. It is so counter to today's culture, and you may, right this moment, be thinking of reasonable objections, but please take a deep breath. Write down any resistance you feel to this concept, and then ask God to help you keep an open mind and show you the truth.

Submission in Christ

Viewing others as more important than yourself does not mean lying down so everyone can walk all over you. It does not mean spending all your time and energy meeting everyone else's needs until there is nothing left of you. Take care to not equate utter exhaustion with humble, selfless serving. God created us to serve and to submit, yes— but in a way that honors Him.

Carolyn Custis James writes in *When Life and Beliefs Collide* that

> Christian submission, which finds its ultimate example in Christ, is an act of strength, understanding, and determination…The believer's call to submission—in the church, the home, in the workplace, or to government officials— is never to a blind or unthinking submission. It carries a heavy responsibility to know, approve, and pursue what is pleasing to God…Unthinking submission is risky business both for the one who submits and the one who leads. [3]

An attitude of submission is absolutely essential to a healthy commitment to God and to another person. Commitment and submission go hand in hand. Healthy commitment gives birth to a desire to submit—to put another's desire above your own. And as in everything else, Jesus set the example of total submission for us.

As we read further in Philippians 2, what do verses 5-8 (page 900) say?

When you really stop and think about this it's absolutely staggering. Jesus is God! He created the universe and controls everything in it. He created us, and yet He submitted Himself to human limitations. Not only did He submit Himself to our limitations, He submitted Himself to the horror and humiliation of crucifixion—a criminal's punishment—so we could share fully in His inheritance. Such submission seems incomprehensible, and yet He did it because He was committed to doing whatever was necessary to bring us into relationship with Him. *Commitment, submission,* and *relationship*. Those three words together form a sacred and beautiful picture of God's perfect plan for our lives.

Husbands and Wives

When you take that picture and apply it to the marriage relationship you have a God-blessed liaison that enables both parties to become more fully the person they were designed to be. Neither side puts their desire first nor has an attitude of greater importance; both work together for mutual benefit.

The Bible addresses the marriage relationship several times.

For example, read the following verses and note what they say.

Ephesians 5:21-33 (page 898)

Love and respect. These are essential elements to a healthy relationship between equal partners intent on putting the other first. One of the best pieces of advice I've heard for a healthy marriage is, regardless of how you feel toward your spouse on any given day, you should still wake up each morning and ask yourself what you can do to make your spouse's day better. That's a good application of Philippians 2:3, which we read earlier.

In some marriages, one person may be an unbeliever. In this case, if the believing spouse determines to reflect Christ in the relationship, it can be used by God as a means through which the unbelieving spouse may be drawn to Him. For example, read aloud what 1 Peter 3:1-2 (page 935) says: *"Your godly lives will speak to them without any words. They will be won over by observing your pure and reverent lives."* Also read 1 Corinthians 7:12-16 (pages 873-874).

In every aspect of the marital relationship, if we determine to develop the attitude of Christ and seek the best for our spouse, we will keep ourselves open to God's fullest blessing in our lives. When we feel taken advantage of, unappreciated, dissatisfied, or restless, it is usually because our focus has slipped from Him and onto ourselves or our circumstances.

Christians are told to *"search for peace, and work to maintain it"* (1 Peter 3:11, page 936). This work as a peacemaker—instead of walking on eggshells in false "peacekeeping" or habitually and fearfully sweeping conflict under the rug—*is* work.

What do the following verses say about humbly speaking truth, even unpopular truth, and living transparently?

1 Peter 3:10 (page 936)

Ephesians 4:15 (page 897)

Colossians 3:9 (page 903)

God tells you that you are precious, honored, and loved by Him. As your focus remains on Him (rather than on how your spouse disappoints you, for example), you will discover that His love satisfies and fills the empty places left by any disappointment.

One loving and respectful thing you can do for your spouse is to pray for them. Pray for their emotional and physical well-being, pray for their spiritual growth, and pray that you will treat them in a way that honors God.

Parents and Children

The next relationship Paul addresses is in Colossians 3:20-21 (page 904).

Why do you think obedience is so important in a child's life?

Obedience is essential to children's physical and emotional well-being. It is foundational to their learning to respect parents and other authority figures. Obedience is so important that God attached a promise to it. Read Ephesians 6:1-3 (page 898).

What is the promise that accompanies an obedient attitude?

As children, if we struggle with obedience to our parents, it can lead to further struggle with obedience to any authority we encounter, including God. The earlier a child learns to submit to authority, the better life will be.

What are parents told to do in Proverbs 22:6 (page 496)?

Parents play a huge part in a child's learning to obey. What does Colossians 3:21 warn against?

Parents who live well-disciplined lives that honor God and set an example for their children will be better able to lovingly and wisely guide and correct their children.

The only way we can direct our children in the right path is if we are walking on the right path ourselves. If we pick and choose which part of God's Word we are going to follow, our children will do the same. If they see us compromise in one area, chances are they will compromise as well. More often than not, a child's area of weakness reflects our own areas of weakness, perhaps with a little different twist.

If you are a parent, in what ways do you see your weaknesses reflected in your children? In what ways do you see your parents' weaknesses reflected in your own life?

What are some things you can do to address this in both your life and theirs?

Just as in a marriage relationship, an important thing you can do for your children (or nieces and nephews, or grandchildren) is to pray for them. Ask God for wisdom and insight in teaching them. Ask Him to show you where and how to improve your parenting skills and strengthen your relationship with your child.

Slaves and Masters

The last relationship Paul addresses is in Colossians 3:22–4:1 (page 904).

At the time Paul wrote Colossians, there were millions of slaves in the Roman Empire. Many of them were acquired through victories in war. Some slaves were well-educated people who became teachers to their owners' children. Though our culture today is quite different, this passage is still rich in applicable truths.

How do you think these verses apply to our culture today?

Do you see how they focus on attitude? Verse 23 is a key verse, telling us to do everything willingly as if we were doing it for God. Remember this refers to the slave-master relationship. What a slave did for the owner was for the owner's well-being. But God says not to look at it that way. Do it willingly, as if for Him. Have Him in mind instead of the owner.

And what does it say He will do in return?

Yes! He'll reward you. And His rewards are nothing to take lightly! In other words, any act of service we do, no matter how offensive or unpleasant, no matter how much we dislike the person who assigned us the task, do it willingly as if we were doing it for God! Think of this in terms that apply to us today.

For example, in the employer-employee relationship. As an employee we are to be dependable, honest, and loyal. We are to work hard whether our boss is watching or not. By the same token, employers are to be just and fair to their employees, treating them with respect and generosity; they are to be concerned about safety precautions, good working conditions, and the well-being of each person.

This is what you have to keep in mind: all biblical teaching has to do with how we think and behave—*not how others behave toward us*. This passage does not say we behave like this only for good and kind employers or hard-working, honest employees. As God enables us, we behave like this regardless of the other person's behavior toward us, obeying God and bringing Him glory.

In All Relationships, We Belong to the Lord

In all of our relationships and interactions with other people, our attitude and behavior should not be based in how they treat us. It should be based in a desire to honor God in everything we do. This does not mean letting people take advantage of you or abuse you.

It means letting God guide your actions and reactions, submitting your thoughts to Him and letting Him be the filter for the words that come from your mouth.

Sometimes it may be necessary to remove yourself from a situation or relationship. When this is the case, do it without bitterness or anger. Do it without speaking derogatorily about the other person, and resist the desire to seek revenge. All of these emotions damage *you* the most—not the other person. If you set your mind to honor God in every circumstance and relationship, even when you are desperately wronged you will come out better and more like Christ. It may take a fair amount of time. It may seem like God isn't coming through, *but He always does*! Focus on Him and keep doing the next right thing.

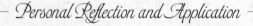

Personal Reflection and Application

From this chapter,

I see...

I believe...

I will...

❧

Prayer

Lord, I will trust in you with all my heart and not depend on my own understanding. I will seek your will in all I do and trust you to show me which path to take. I know that I can do everything you ask of me because you give me strength. You are my refuge and strength and are always ready to help me in times of trouble (Proverbs 3:5-6, page 482; Philippians 4:13, page 901; and Psalm 46:1, page 434).

———— *Thoughts, Notes, and Prayer Requests* ————

_____

_____

_____

_____

_____

_____

_____

_____

_____

_____

_____

_____

_____

7

Christ and Others

Colossians 4:2-18

In her younger years, my friend Sandee decided to move to Hawaii with a friend. They'd both been raised in Michigan with its long, raw winters and wanted to experience a more moderate climate. Upon their arrival, they found living expenses to be very high and had to find a couple of other girls to share rent.

Sandee found one of their new roommates very difficult to get along with. Their personalities were different, as were their tastes, habits, and lifestyles. They argued at every turn. Sandee grew more and more miserable as her living conditions became more intolerable.

She pleaded with God to help her get along with her roommate better, but every day was a struggle. One day God planted the thought in her mind to treat the other young woman as if she were her best friend. Instead of avoiding her she invited her to do things with her. Instead of sharp retorts and critical comments, she complimented her and purposely engaged her in conversation. The woman was puzzled by the change in her roommate and gradually began to respond more positively.

One day, when Sandee invited the woman to come on an outing, she realized she sincerely looked forward to spending the time with her, and she enjoyed the whole day. She didn't have to bite her tongue once! By the time Sandee decided to move back to Michigan, she and her roommate had become true friends—a friendship that has endured for more than 40 years.

Prayer

God, rid me of all bitterness, rage, anger, harsh words, and slander, as well as all types of evil behavior. Help me instead be kind to others, tenderhearted, and forgiving, just as you have forgiven me. Help me show deep love for others, for love covers a multitude of sins. I know that when my life pleases you, you make even my enemies to be at peace with me. Help me to always do to others what I would like them to do to me (Ephesians 4:31-32, page 897; 1 Peter 4:8, page 936; Proverbs 16:7, page 492; and Matthew 7:12a, page 738).

Characteristics of Our New Way of Life

The apostle Paul continues to point us toward a better way of life found through a personal relationship with Jesus Christ. In the fourth chapter of Colossians, Paul concludes his letter with some final and important instructions in living obedient, fulfilling, productive lives as Christians.

Conversation with God

What is Paul's first instruction in Colossians 4:2 (page 904)?

Prayer is vital to our relationship with God. It keeps us connected with Him so our hearts and minds are in tune with His. Prayer should not be something we resort to only when the going gets tough. It should be a delightful, enriching, ongoing communication with the One who loves us more than we can ever comprehend. James 5:16b (pages 932-933) says, *"The earnest prayer of a righteous person has great power and produces wonderful results."* God wants us to come to Him with any and all situations. We have the Holy Spirit in us, directing us to pray as He leads. That is where the power comes from! That makes our prayers effective!

To not develop the habit of prayer is like being given access to an unlimited bank account and refusing to spend any of the money. Prayer is quite literally our lifeline!

What principles regarding prayer do the following verses teach?

Ephesians 6:18 (page 898)

1 Thessalonians 5:16-18 (page 907)

Philippians 4:6-7 (page 901)

Both Colossians 4:2 and Ephesians 6:18 talk about prayer and staying alert. What connection do you see between the two?

Did you notice that Colossians 4:2 and two of the three passages above combine prayer and thankfulness? Why do you think that connection is significant?

Closeness to God

Think of your closest relationship. How often do you communicate with that person?

What do you talk about?

If you have a personal relationship with God, you will want to communicate regularly with Him—about everything. If you only come to Him with your problems, you shortchange the most significant relationship in your life!

"Those persons who know the deep peace of God, the unfathomable peace that passeth all understanding, are always men and women of much prayer."
—R.A. Torrey

Have you ever had a relationship with someone who only got in touch with you when they needed something? How did you feel about that person?

God isn't interested in a genie-in-a-bottle, make-a-wish relationship. He wants to be an integral and significant part of our lives, and that only happens through frequent and intimate communication. Prayer isn't a vague, mystical ritual that connects us to a distant, unapproachable god. Prayer breathes life and authenticity into our relationship with God. It is one means by which we are transformed into His image, causing our heart and mind to resonate with His.

Praying in Faith and Obedience

What do the following verses have in common regarding the topic of prayer?

1 John 5:14-15 (pages 943-944)

1 John 3:21-23 (pages 942-943)

John 14:13 (page 823)

What are the two cautions about answered prayer?

1.

2.

Obedience and asking in Jesus' name are closely connected. To ask in Jesus' name acknowledges His authority and will. When we recognize and honor God's authority in our lives, we obey Him, and our will aligns with His will. As a result, our desires will begin to match His. What we ask for will not be for selfish benefit but for His honor.

There is another important aspect to prayer.

What characteristic must we also have when we pray, according to James 1:6-8 (page 930)?

God wants us to come fully trusting Him, being confident that He will answer us. We can miss out on experiencing His answer to prayer when our faith bounces between trusting Him fully and putting our trust in circumstances or someone else.

What is an area in which you need to put your faith in God rather than trusting in your own or someone else's ability?

I most often struggled with leaving things completely in God's hands during the years we raised our two sons. So often I trusted my love for them more than His love for them and stepped in when I should have stepped back.

There is so much to learn about prayer and so many resources on prayer available to us. One of the best ways to learn about prayer is to do it. It is not complicated or difficult, and it doesn't require following a formula. It is just talking and listening to God. And like all communication, the more you do it, the easier and more natural it becomes.

The Prayers of the Apostle Paul

Paul spent years in prison and a good amount of that time he spent in prayer. Following are four of those prayers.

As you read them, record what Paul specifically prays for in each one.

Ephesians 1:15-23 (page 895)

Ephesians 3:14-21 (page 896)

Philippians 1:9-11 (page 899)

Colossians 1:9-12 (page 902)

Each prayer was for the spiritual growth and joy of other believers! Even in the circumstances of imprisonment, Paul's thoughts are on others, not himself. It's a good example for us to follow. In fact, how about if we try it? Think of someone you'd like to pray one of these prayers for. Copy it on a card, personalizing it for them, and then pray for them daily, using one of Paul's prayers as your guide. Watch to see various ways in which God answers your prayer.

Praying About the Proclamation of God's Message

Paul didn't just pray for other believers. He wisely made them a part of his life by asking them to pray for him also. Read Colossians 4:3-4 (page 904).

What strikes you about Paul's personal prayer request?

What strikes me is that there is no mention of his physical well-being. He wants only to be able to clearly proclaim the Gospel of Jesus to everyone he meets!

When Paul talks about "proclaiming this message," what do you think he means?

Paul experienced a total transformation as a result of his relationship with Jesus Christ. The message that transformed his life is that Jesus died for his sins and came back to life three days later—so Paul could know Him personally and have eternal life with Him in heaven after he died. Once Paul met Jesus and experienced that transformation, he wanted everyone else to experience it as well. It became the driving force of his life for the rest of his time on earth.

Prayer brings us close to God. And praying for others, called intercession, impacts the people you pray for, which in turns impacts the people around them. As we pray for our families, friends, co-workers, and other believers, we impact their lives in a special way. When we expand our intercessory prayer to include the leaders of our country and our world, we bring God's power into areas we ourselves could never go. There is no barrier in this world that our prayers cannot penetrate. Never be fooled into thinking your prayers don't make a difference. They do!

Years ago I began praying for our entertainment industry because I believe it, more than anything else, determines the morals of our culture. Every time I hear of an entertainer coming to Christ I rejoice over God's answers to prayer. When movies come out that promote Christian values, I know it's an answer to prayer.

I've started keeping a file of these answers, and I can't help but weep with each article or blurb I add to it. Just this week I read an incredible article about a popular TV star's conversion to Christ. It's amazing how often I become aware of such news, now that I'm tuned into it. God is always working in response to our prayers. Don't think you're not making a difference, and don't get discouraged.

Our Influence on Those Who Are Not Believers

Colossians 4:5-6 (page 904) tells us how to live influential lives for God.

What parts of your life line up with these instructions? What must change?

Wise and gracious. Can there be a more appealing combination? People are drawn to wisdom; they are disarmed by graciousness. When we live wisely and graciously, our lives will be an effective witness for Jesus.

How does Colossians 4:5-6 compare to 1 Peter 3:15-16 (page 936)?

This passage in 1 Peter is significant, especially if you're hesitant about sharing your faith. Verse 15 says to "*always be ready*." One of the reasons it can be intimidating to share our faith is because we're usually not prepared. If you have your answer ready ahead of time and know exactly what you want to say when the opportunity arises, it will take much of the fear out of it.

Preparing an Answer for Those Who Ask

Putting together your faith story is simple. Just ask yourself three questions:

1. What was your life like before Christ? What ongoing weakness or struggle often resulted in poor decisions? (For example, insecurities caused you to compromise your values, a need to be in control prompted anger or caused you to hold on too tightly to things.)

2. How did you come to Christ? What attracted you to Him? Who told you about Him? What was going on in your life at the time you put your trust in Him?

3. How is your life different as a result of your relationship to God? What are the benefits? How does knowing Him help you respond in a healthy way to the weakness or struggle you mentioned in the first question?

Keep your answers brief and to the point, without excessive details. Hone them down to where you can share your faith story in two to three minutes. When you have it so you're saying exactly what you want to say, practice it until you feel comfortable.

Your story most likely will be a little different each time you share it. As you become comfortable talking about spiritual things with others, you will be able to better adapt your story to your audience. Write out your faith story this week, and next time we're together we can share them with each other.

Greetings from Paul and His Fellow Workers

In the last verses of this chapter, Paul talks about some specific believers.

As you read Colossians 4:7-14 (page 904) note below the different ways he refers to them.

Did you see how lovingly and respectfully he talked about them? These people, like Paul, had all been transformed by their relationship with Christ. They experienced persecution in various forms, but remained focused on God and did all they could to encourage each other. I think you'll find their brief biographies interesting:

- *Tychicus*, a Christian from the Roman province of Asia (now part of Turkey), traveled with Paul as his faithful co-worker and became a representative for Paul to various churches.

- *Onesimus* was slave to a man named Philemon. He fled to Rome, possibly after stealing money or property from his owner. While on the run he met Paul, who told him about Jesus. Onesimus became a committed follower of Jesus, devoted to helping Paul. Paul would have loved for his new brother to stay with him in Rome, but he knew Onesimus needed to make things right with his owner. Paul wrote a letter to Philemon on his behalf. He told him that Onesimus had become a Christian and asked him to receive the man back as a Christian brother and not as a slave. Onesimus and Tychicus delivered the letter to Philemon. Imagine the courage it took for Onesimus to go back. You can read Paul's amazing letter in the book of Philemon (page 919).

- *Aristarchus* was a loyal co-worker of Paul and came from Thessalonica. He was captured in Ephesus during the riot against Christians. At the time this letter was written he was sharing Paul's imprisonment.

- *Mark* had joined Paul and Barnabas on a mission trip but deserted them in the middle of it. On their second mission trip, Barnabas wanted to take Mark along again. Paul sharply disagreed because of Mark's former desertion. As a result, Paul and Barnabas went on two separate trips (Acts 15:36-39, page 844). Thankfully, over time Mark grew, and Paul recognized his full potential as a ministry helper (2 Timothy 4:11, page 916). Mark is well-known as the author of the second book of the New Testament.

- *Epaphras* is the man we learned about when we began this study. He founded the church in Colosse and traveled to Rome to visit Paul in prison. He was a fervent man of intercessory prayer who worked hard to bring the Gospel to Colosse, Laodicea, and Hierapolis. If you recall, it was Epaphras who had acquainted Paul with the conditions that motivated the apostle to write this letter.

- *Luke*, a physician, wrote the third book of the New Testament as well as the book of Acts. He was a Gentile who joined Paul on his second missionary trip and was the only companion who stayed with Paul to the end of his Roman imprisonment.

- *Demas* was another co-worker. Sadly, after this letter was written, he was enticed back to his former life and deserted Paul.

After his specific greetings, Paul passes on general greetings. Read Colossians 4:15-18 (page 904).

Only at the very end does Paul reference his physical circumstances. *"Remember my chains."* Somehow that simple sentence, devoid of adjectives, speaks volumes. He consistently lived what he preached, focusing on God and not on his circumstances. In Paul we see the kind of incredible, influential life of one who was fully committed to Christ.

How encouraging it must have been for the Colossians to receive this letter! Can you imagine how the word spread among them? *"Did you hear? A letter's just arrived from Paul! Let's get together and read it!"* Can you imagine them gathered together listening intently to his encouraging words. Do you suppose they prayed together when it was finished? Do you think they encouraged each other and renewed their commitment to the pure truth of God's Word?

What about you? How have Paul's words encouraged and convicted you? Take a moment to list any specific changes God is leading you to make as a result of studying Paul's letter to the Colossians.

Consider asking a friend to regularly check in with you on how you are growing in these areas.

There can be no better way to conclude this study than with Paul's own words: *"May God's grace be with you."* What a wonderful word—*grace*. Within that one word is contained all of God's favor and blessing, all of His love expressed through the gift of salvation.

Don't forget to write out your faith story this week!

—————— *Personal Reflection and Application* ——————

From this chapter,

I see...

I believe...

I will...

Prayer

Lord, how wonderful to know that I can come boldly to your throne, where I will receive your mercy and find grace to help me when I need it most. You are so rich in mercy, and you loved me so much that even though I was dead because of my sins, you gave me life when you raised Christ from the dead. (It is only by your grace that I have been saved!) I am an example of the incredible wealth of your grace and kindness toward me, shown in all you have done for me since I became united with Christ Jesus. You saved me by your grace when I believed. And I can't take credit for this; it is a gift from you. My salvation is not a reward for the good things I have done, so I cannot boast about it. I give thanks to you, for you are good and your faithful love endures forever (Hebrews 4:16, page 922; Ephesians 2:4-5,7-9, pages 895-896; and Psalm 118:29, page 468).

Thoughts, Notes, and Prayer Requests

_____

_____

_____

_____

_____

_____

_____

_____

8

Sharing Faith Stories

My Faith Story

My father died when I was very young. As a result of his death, a cloud of impending doom settled over my head, and I went through life always expecting the worst to happen. I held back from forming close relationships, unable to trust that they would last. I lived a skin-deep life, and joy was a foreign concept.

One day a teacher told me that God loved me and that it was a love I could count on. I didn't have to worry about God leaving or hurting me. In fact, she told me He so wanted a relationship with me that He'd sent His Son, Jesus, to die for my sins. She assured me that if I'd just give Him a chance, I'd discover how much more there was to life than what I was experiencing.

The day I committed my life to God was even more life-changing than the day my father died. God completely obliterated that cloud of impending doom that shadowed my life, and He opened my eyes to an exquisite spectrum of unimaginable color. My relationship with Him is an incredible, ongoing process where He continually keeps reminding me He's never going to leave—even when life gets really hard. He assures me that He has a wonderful plan for my life, so every morning I wake up with an energizing sense of anticipation for what the day holds. In the long run, God always exceeds my expectations.

Prayer

Lord, you have said that as iron sharpens iron, so a friend sharpens a friend. Help me to be the kind of person who motivates others to acts of love and good works. Help me to encourage the people around me and build them up. Help me to share their burdens, knowing that this is the way to obey your law. Finally, let me be of one mind with other believers, sympathizing with them, loving them as brothers and sisters, and being tenderhearted with a humble attitude. I want to imitate you, God, in everything I do, because I am your child. I want to live a life filled with love, following the example of Christ, who loved me and offered Himself as a sacrifice for me (Proverbs 27:17, page 501; Hebrews 10:24, page 926; 1 Thessalonians 5:11, page 907; Galatians 6:2, page 894; 1 Peter 3:8, page 936; and Ephesians 5:1-2, page 897).

Sharing the Wonder of Christ in Us

In this study we discovered a very important theme: Christ's supremacy! As the visible image of God, Christ existed before anything was created—and He is in and through everything. And we learned that everything was created for Him! That includes you and me.

In Christ lives the fullness of God. Because of this, we are complete when we are united with Him. What an amazing thought that everything we need can be found in Him. And because He resides within us, we have the privilege of sharing His story with others.

Paul urged the Colossians to be bold in sharing their faith. God wants all of His followers to do the same. In the last chapter we were given three questions to help each of us write out our own faith story in a simple, easy-to-share format. Let's practice boldness by sharing our faith story with each other. You don't have to, of course, but be open to the possibility as you listen to others share their stories.

(Allow time to share faith stories.)

It's encouraging to hear others' faith stories. And this I know: God is proud of you for putting your story together! He's proud of you for having the courage to share it—and this is just the beginning. Now that you have prepared your faith story, He will help you *"make the most of every opportunity"* (Colossians 4:5, page 904). Let's close our time together by asking Him to give us both boldness and opportunities to share our faith story with others.

(Prayer)

What a wonderful experience it has been to go through this study together! I look forward to meeting you in another study sometime, and until we do, may God's grace be with you!

—————— *Thoughts, Notes, and Prayer Requests* ——————

_____

_____

_____

_____

_____

_____

_____

_____

Journal Pages

Know God

It does not matter what has happened in your past. No matter what you've done, no matter how you've lived your life,

God is personally interested in you right now.
He cares about you.

God understands your frustration, your loneliness, your heartaches. He wants each of us to come to Him, to know Him personally.

God is so rich in mercy, and he loved us so much,
that even though we were dead because of our sins,
he gave us life when he raised Christ from the dead.
(It is only by God's grace that you have been saved!)

—Ephesians 2:4-5 (page 895)

God loves you.

He created you in His image. His desire is to be in relationship with you. He wants you to belong to Him.

Sadly, our sin gets in the way. It separates us from God, and without Him we are dead in our spirits. There is nothing we can do to close that gap. There is nothing we can do to give ourselves life. No matter how well we may behave.

But God loves us so much that He made a way to eliminate that gap and give us new life, His kind of life—to restore the relationship. His love for us is so great, so tremendous, that He sent Jesus Christ, His only Son, to earth to live, and then die—filling the gap and taking the punishment we deserve for refusing God's ways.

God made Christ, who never sinned, to be the offering for our sin,
so that we could be made right with God through Christ.

—2 Corinthians 5:21 (page 884)

Jesus Christ, God's Son, not only died to pay the penalty for your sin, but He conquered death when He rose from the grave. He is ready to share His life with you.

**Christ reconciles us to God. Jesus is alive today.
He will give you a new beginning and a newly created life
when you surrender control of your life to Him.**

Anyone who belongs to Christ has become a new person.
The old life is gone; a new life has begun!

—2 Corinthians 5:17 (page 884)

How do you begin this new life? You need to realize

...the necessity of repenting from sin and turning to God,
and of having faith in our Lord Jesus.

—Acts 20:21 (page 849)

Agree with God about your sins and believe that Jesus came to save you, that He is your Savior and Lord. Ask Him to lead your life.

God loved the world so much that he gave his one and only Son,
so that everyone who believes in him will not perish but have
eternal life. God sent his Son into the world not to judge the world,
but to save the world through him.
—John 3:16-17 (page 811)

Pray something like this:

Jesus, I do believe you are the Son of God and that you died on the cross to pay the penalty for my sin. Forgive me. I turn away from my sin and choose to live a life that pleases you. Enter my life as my Savior and Lord.

I want to follow you and make you the leader of my life.

Thank you for your gift of eternal life and for the Holy Spirit, who has now come to live in me. I ask this in your name. Amen.

God puts His Spirit inside you, who enables you to live a life pleasing to Him. He gives you new life that will never die, that will last forever—eternally.

When you surrender your life to Jesus Christ, you are making the most important decision of your life. Stonecroft would like to offer you a free download of *A New Beginning*, a short Bible study that will help you as you begin your new life in Christ. Go to **stonecroft.org/newbeginning**.

If you'd like to talk with someone right now about this prayer, call **1.888.NEED.HIM**.

Who Is Stonecroft?

Every day Stonecroft communicates the Gospel in meaningful ways. Whether side by side with a neighbor or new friend, or through a speaker sharing her transformational story, the Gospel of Jesus Christ goes forward. Through a variety of outreach activities and small group Bible studies specifically designed for those not familiar with God, and with online and print resources focused on evangelism, Stonecroft proclaims the Gospel of Jesus Christ to women where they are, as they are.

For more than 75 years, always with a foundation of prayer in reliance on God, Stonecroft volunteers have found ways to introduce women to Jesus Christ and train them to share His Good News with others.

Stonecroft understands and appreciates the influence of one woman's life. When you reach her, you touch everyone she knows—her family, friends, neighbors, and co-workers. The real Truth of the Gospel brings real redemption into real lives.

Our life-changing, faith-building community resources include:

- ***Stonecroft Bible and Book Studies***—both topical and chapter-by-chapter studies. We designed Stonecroft studies for those in small groups—those who know Christ and those who do not yet know Him—to simply yet profoundly discover God's Word together.

- ***Stonecroft Prays!***—calls small groups of women together to pray for God to show them avenues to reach women in their community with the Gospel.

- ***Outreach Events***—set the stage for women to hear and share the Gospel with their communities. Whether in a large venue, workshop, or small group setting, Stonecroft women find ways to share the love of Christ.

- ***Stonecroft Military***—a specialized effort to honor women connected to the U.S. military and share the Gospel with them while showing them the love of Christ.

- ***Small Group Studies for Christians***—these resources reveal God's heart for those who do not yet know Him. The Aware Series includes *Aware, Belong*, and *Call*.

- ***Stonecroft Life Publications***—clearly explain the Gospel through stories of people whose lives have been transformed by Jesus Christ.

- ***Stonecroft.org***—offers fresh content daily to equip and encourage you.

Dedicated and enthusiastic Stonecroft staff serve you via Divisional Field Directors stationed across the United States, and a Home Office team who support tens of thousands of dedicated volunteers worldwide.

Your life matters. Join us today to impact your communities with the Gospel of Jesus Christ. Become involved with Stonecroft.

STONECROFT

| Get started:
connections@stonecroft.org
800.525.8627 | Support Stonecroft:
stonecroft.org/donate | Order resources:
stonecroft.org/store
888.819.5218 |

Books for Further Study

Eggerichs, Dr. Emerson. *The Language of Love & Respect.* Nashville, TN: Thomas Nelson Publishers, 2009.

Ferguson, Everett. *Backgrounds of Early Christianity, 3rd ed.* Grand Rapids, MI: Wm. B. Eerdmans Publishing Co., 2003.

Garland, David E. *The NIV Application Commentary.* Grand Rapids, MI: Zondervan Publishing House, 1998.

James, Carolyn Custis. *When Life and Beliefs Collide.* Grand Rapids, MI: Zondervan, 2001.

Keller, Timothy and Kathy. *The Meaning of Marriage.* New York: Dutton, Penguin Group, 2011.

McDowell, Josh. *The New Evidence That Demands a Verdict.* Nashville, TN: Thomas Nelson Publishers, 1999.

Pollock, John. *The Apostle: A Life of Paul.* Colorado Springs, CO: David C. Cook, 2012.

Notes

1. David E. Garland, *The NIV Application Commentary* (Grand Rapids, MI: Zondervan Publishing House, 1998), p. 224.

2. Garland, p. 243.

3. Carolyn Custis James, *When Life and Beliefs Collide* (Grand Rapids, MI: Zondervan, 2001), p. 50.

Stonecroft Resources

Stonecroft Bible Studies make the Word of God accessible to everyone. These studies allow small groups to discover the adventure of a personal relationship with God and introduce others to God's unlimited love, grace, forgiveness, and power. To learn more, visit **stonecroft.org/biblestudies**.

Who Is Jesus? (6 chapters)

He was a rebel against the status quo. The religious community viewed Him as a threat. The helpless and outcast considered Him a friend. Explore the life and teachings of Jesus—this rebel with a cause who challenges us today to a life of radical faith.

What Is God Like? (6 chapters)

What is God like? Is He just a higher power? Has He created us and left us on our own? Where is He when things don't make sense? Discover what the Bible tells us about God and how we can know Him in a life-transforming way.

Who Is the Holy Spirit? (6 chapters)

Are you living up to the full life that God wants for you? Learn about the Holy Spirit, our Helper and power source for everyday living, who works in perfect harmony with God the Father and Jesus the Son.

Connecting with God (8 chapters)

Prayer is our heart-to-heart communication with our heavenly Father. This study examines the purpose, power, and elements of prayer, sharing biblical principles for effective prayer.

Today I Pray

When we bow before God on behalf of someone who doesn't yet know of His saving work, of His great love in sending His Son Jesus, of His mercy and goodness, we enter into a work that has eternal impact. Stonecroft designed *Today I Pray* as a 30-day intercessory prayer commitment that you may use to focus your prayers on behalf of a specific person, or to pray for many—because your prayers are powerful and important!

Prayer Worth Repeating (15 devotions)

There is no place where your prayers to the one and only God cannot penetrate, no circumstance prayers cannot impact. As the mother of adult children, your greatest influence into their lives is through prayer. *Prayer Worth Repeating* is a devotional prayer guide designed to focus your prayers and encourage you to trust God more deeply as He works in the lives of your adult children.

Pray & Play Devotional (12 devotions)

It's playgroup with a purpose! Plus Mom tips. For details on starting a Pray & Play group, visit **stonecroft.org/prayandplay** or call **800.525.8627**.

Prayer Journal

A practical resource to strengthen your prayer life, this booklet includes an introductory section about the importance of prayer, the basic elements of prayer and a clear Gospel presentation, as well as 40 pages of journaling your prayer requests and God's answers.

Prayer—Talking with God

This booklet provides insight and biblical principles to help you establish a stronger, more effective prayer life.

Aware (5 lessons)

Making Jesus known every day starts when we are *Aware* of those around us. This dynamic Stonecroft Small Group Bible Study about "Always Watching and Responding with Encouragement" equips and engages people in the initial steps to the joys of evangelism.

Belong (6 lessons)

For many in today's culture, the desire to belong is often part of their journey to believe. *Belong* explores how we can follow in Jesus' footsteps—and walk with others on their journey to belong.

Call (7 lessons)

Every day we meet people without Christ. That is God's intention. He wants His people to initiate and build friendships. He wants us together. *Call* helps us take a closer look at how God makes Himself known through our relationships with those around us. Discover together God's clear calling for you and those near to you.

Order these and other Stonecroft Resources
at our online store at **stonecroft.org/store**

If you have been encouraged and brought closer to God by this study, please consider giving a gift to Stonecroft so that others can experience life change as well. You can find information about giving online at **stonecroft.org**. (Click on the "Donate" tab.)

If you'd like to give via telephone, please contact us at **800.525.8627**. Or you can mail your gift to

Stonecroft
10561 Barkley, Suite 500
Overland Park, KS 66212

STONECROFT

10561 Barkley, Suite 500, Overland Park, KS 66212
Telephone: 800.525.8627
E-mail: connections@stonecroft.org
stonecroft.org

Abundant Life Bible
New Living Translation Holy Bible

*Experience the presence of God
in everyday life*

Stonecroft is pleased to partner with
Tyndale to offer the New Living
Translation Holy Bible as the
companion for our newly released
Stonecroft Bible Studies.

The New Living Translation translators set out to render the message of the original
Scripture language texts into clear, contemporary English. In this *translation*, scholars kept
the concerns of both formal-equivalence and dynamic-equivalence in mind. Their
goal was a Bible that is faithful to the ancient texts and eminently readable.
The result is a translation that is both accurate and powerful.

TRUTH MADE CLEAR

Features of the Abundant Life Bible

- Features are easy-to-use and written
  for people who don't yet know Jesus
  Christ personally.
- Unequaled clarity and accuracy
- Dictionary included
- Concordance included
- Old Testament included

- Introductory notes on important abundant life
  topics such as:
  Gospel presentation   Practical guidance
  Joy   Life's tough issues
  Peace   Prayer
- Insights from a relationship with Jesus Christ.
- Ideal Scripture text for those not familiar with
  the Bible!

Tyndale House Publishers

To order: stonecroft.org/store
888.819.5218